JACK

and Other New Poems

JACK

and Other New Poems

MAXINE KUMIN

W. W. NORTON & COMPANY

New York   London

Copyright © 2005 by Maxine Kumin

For information about permission to reproduce selections from this book, write to
Permissions, W. W. Norton & Company, Inc., 500 Fifth Avenue, New York, NY 10110

Manufacturing by the Courier Companies, Inc.
Book design by JAM Design
Production manager: Andrew Marasia

Library of Congress Cataloging-in-Publication Data

Kumin, Maxine, date.
Jack and other new poems / Maxine Kumin.— 1st ed.
p. cm.
ISBN 0-393-05956-1 (hardcover)
I. Title.
PS3521.U638J33 2005
811'.54—dc22

2004021762

W. W. Norton & Company, Inc.
500 Fifth Avenue, New York, N.Y. 10110
www.wwnorton.com

W. W. Norton & Company Ltd.
Castle House, 75/76 Wells Street, London W1T 3QT

1 2 3 4 5 6 7 8 9 0

To Danny and Libby

CONTENTS

I

THE HIGHWAYMEN

It's true: you wake up one morning and they're gone,
the flock of a hundred redpolls who swept in like Huns
with their tiny red caps and black mustaches,
their breasts freckled and stippled like thrushes',
an irruption of redpolls you haven't seen in a decade
and may never see again in the disorderly parade
of your lifetime. How they intimidated the chickadees,
the titmice, even the needle-nosed nuthatches,
batting your year-round faithfuls away from the feeder.
How they chattered, snatching and flapping, rapacious
yet charming in their little red yarmulkas . . .
you shiver, remembering, refilling the cylinder.
The sunflower seeds glisten like ebony.
O merciless January, where have the highwaymen gone?

It's snowing again.
All day, reruns
of the blizzard of '78
newscasters vying
for bragging rights
how it was to go hungry
after they'd thumped
the vending machines empty
the weatherman clomping
four miles on snowshoes
to get to his mike
so he could explain
how three lows
could collide to create
a lineup of isobars
footage of state troopers
peering into the caked
windows of cars
backed up for white
miles on the interstate.

No reruns today
of the bombings in Vietnam
2 million civilians blown
apart, most of them children
under 16, children

always the least
able to dive
for cover when
all that tonnage bursts
from a blind sky.
Snow here is
weighting the pine trees
while we wait for the worst:
for war to begin.
Schools closed, how
the children
love a benign blizzard
a downhill scrimmage
of tubes and sleds. But who
remembers the blizzard
that burst on those other children?
Back then we called it
collateral damage
and will again.

FOX ON HIS BACK

homage to Theodore Roethke

On long nights shy of melt
implacable and clear
wind drilling the last leaf
the poet to play it safe
slept with a baby's quilt
pulled over his bald head.
O what's the winter for?
To remember love, he said.

Fox on his back in a hole
snake eyes in the wall asleep
grubs shellacked in their coils
sap locked tight to the pith
roots sucking a hollow tooth
a brown and pregnant bear
leaf-wrapped like an old cigar. . . .

O what's the winter for?
the quilted poet asked.
Doors slam overhead
as maple buffets ash.
To remember love, he said.

WIDOW AND DOG

After he died she started letting the dog
sleep on his side of the bed they had shared
for fifty-one years. A large discreet dog, he stayed
on his side but the tags on his collar jingled as he sighed
and especially when he scratched so she took his collar off
and then his smooth tawny bulk close to her but not
touching eased her through the next night and the next.

One morning, a chipmunk and his wife somehow slipped in
through the screen door when neither of them was looking.
She got up screaming from her coffee and whacked at them
with a broom. Dog pounced and pounced but they were faster
than he was and dove under the refrigerator. After a while
he stopped crashing into chairs and skidding around corners
in fruitless pursuit and then they came and went untroubled
even drinking out of his water dish, their tails at right angles.

That summer it just seemed simpler to leave the window
by the bird feeder open for ease of refilling. Some creatures
slipped casually out and in. The titmice were especially graceful.
She loved to watch them elevate and retract their crests
whenever they perched on the lips of the kitchen counters.
The goldfinches chittered and sang like drunken canaries
and once in a thunderstorm a barred owl blundered
into that fake crystal chandelier she had always detested.

.   .   .

Autumn fell on them in a joyous rush. The first
needles of hard frost, the newly sharp wind, the final
sweep and swirl of leaves, a swash of all-day rain
were not unwelcome. Hickory nuts ricocheted
off the barn's metal roof like a rain of beebee-gun pellets.
They both took afternoon naps. They both grew portly.
While Dog in his dumb allegiance dozed on the hearth,
sometimes he ran so fiercely in his dreams that he bared
    his teeth.
Reclusive comfortable Widow scribbled in her journal.
It did not matter how much she woolgathered, how late
into the night she read, it did not matter if she
completed this poem, or another.

THE BROTHERS

Whenever I visit my birthplace, the City
of Brotherly Love, where my brothers married
two sisters, I think of Chang and Eng, whose darkling

birth face to face in 1811 was considered
an evil omen foretelling the end of the world.
King Rama the Second, monarch of Siam

ordered them put to death but relented
when the earth stubbornly clung to its orbit.
In time, the twosome learned

to stretch the five-inch ligament that bound
their breastbones together until they could
at least stand side by side, which they did,

touring circuses worldwide, making a living
as P. T. Barnum freaks. They chose to retire
to a little carnival town in North Carolina

where they had once been happy, and where
they met two daughters of a simple farmer.
Upon marriage a bed was custom-made to fit

.   .   .

the foursome and nine months later the wives
gave birth six days apart to daughters. Alas!
The sisters began to bicker, declaring each

one's child was prettier, each was plumper. Soon
the brothers also quarreled. Bitter, bitter
the frustration of it, tied chest to chest,

yet swiping sidewise blows at one another.
Chang took to whiskey to obliterate his anger,
Eng to endless smoke-filled games of poker.

I try to imagine the business of dragging
your drunken living doppelganger
away from bottle to card table and vice

versa. The furious wives I can well imagine.
My brothers, who also married two sisters,
lived in one house in the City of Brotherly Love,

albeit in two beds, and not happily
ever after. Quarrels arose over money
—in fact and fiction it is always over money—

.   .   .

the family silver, as it were. Bitter,
bitter, alas, the brothers struck and swore
not as they had as children, but more subtly.

The sisters swelled empurpled, as in Grimm.
The coming apart was stormy, the paired rages
took down both households, heart and hearthstone.

Chang and Eng, worn by their marital crises,
forfeited the honeymoon cottage, the custom-made bed.
They built two houses a mile apart for the sisters,

spent three days each with each wife
and sired twenty-one children between them.
I do not know if the women ever spoke

to one another again or if they forbade
their offspring, the cousins, to do so. From time
to time the men resumed their carnival tours

as *Remarkable Oddities! Siamese Twins!*
to support their separate households. Years went by
as the brothers trudged their chosen mile. Death

.   .   .

overtook them in their chains without a moment's warning—
a blood clot on Chang's brain, Eng dead of shock or grief
or both two hours later, thereby providing

a sort of Brothers Grimm's macabre moral:
the band of gristle that connects the living
cannot be chewed apart even in dying.

My brothers' sons and daughters, once dear friends,
acquiring little by little their parents' poison,
alas, now no longer mingled.

Alas, two generations later, all,
all remain estranged. In fairy tales
some reckoning would come: the daughters

of the daughters reveal their kinship
in a chance meeting in the castle courtyard,
the brothers' heirs, returning with their yeomen,

cast off their dark disguises and embrace.
But in real life the masque plays out: two brothers
move from love to loathing and die unreconciled.

.   .   .

Their widows are condemned to dine
on plattersful of hate to the end. Doesn't it beg
for a moral, some resolution? I remember

the lion extends his thorny paw to the mouse.
The hunter shoots the wolf who ate Grandmother.
In my account, the cruel king decrees

the infants shall be smothered in their beds
before they can grow up to marry siblings,
but my better self invents a happy ending

in which the brothers die like Chang and Eng,
minutes apart, and everyone—offspring, aunts,
uncles and cousins—comes to a funeral

staged like a sendoff to an adored royal figure,
a banquet with brandy and schnapps, music,
and drunken family members embracing.

THE SUNDAY PHONE CALL

Drab December, sleet falling.
Dogs loosely fisted in torpor.
Horses nose-down in hay.
It's the hour, years ago
I used to call my parents
or they'd call me.

The phone rings. Idly
empty of expectation
I answer. It's my father's
voice. *Pop!* I say, *you're dead!*
Don't you remember
that final heart attack
Dallas, just before
Kennedy was shot?

Time means nothing here,
kiddo. He's jolly, expansive.
You can wait eons for an open line.
Time gets used up but
comes back, you know.
Like Ping-Pong.

Ping-Pong! The table in
the attic. My father, shirtsleeves
rolled, the wet stub of

a burnt-out cigarette
stuck to his lower lip as
he murdered each one
of my three older brothers
and me yearning under the eaves
waiting for my turn.

You sound . . . just like yourself
I say. *I am myself, godammit!*
Anyway, what's this
about an accident?

How did you hear about it?

I read it somewhere. Broke
your neck, etcetera.
He says this vaguely
his shorthand way
of keeping feelings at bay.

You mean you read
my memoir? Did
you know you're in it?

.   .   .

Didn't read that part. No
reason to stir things up.
Now I'm indignant.
But I almost died!

Didn't I tell you
never buy land on a hill?
It's worthless. What's
an educated dame like you
doing messing with horses?
Messing with horses is
for punks. (Then, a little
softer), *I see you two've*
put a lot of work into
that hunk of real estate.

Thanks. Thanks for even
noticing. We love it here.
We'll never sell.

Like hell you won't!
You will!

Pop, I say, tearing up,
let's not fight for once.
My only Poppa, when

do I get to see you?
A long pause. Then
coughing his cigarette cough
Pupchen, he says
I may be dead but
I'm not clairvoyant.
Behave yourself.
The line clicks off.

THE SNARL

10 p.m. A snarl, a voice I recognize almost at once
for hadn't he married a high school classmate, one
of the clique that had snubbed me down to the bone
so that I ate my dry sandwich daily in a stall
in the john after Latin class and bolted from there
to the back of the library's card catalogue?
Aeneas, loitering in Carthage, must not forget
his destiny: he is to found Italy.
Dido must burn on her pyre. Not that

I'd ever seen either one of them since
Cheltenham High but remember thinking when
I saw the wedding notice what an unlikely pair:
she in her pageboy bob, queen of the front row,
chewing forbidden gum, passing notes, swivelling
to aim her triggered breasts at the multitude,
he the louche bad boy in the back row of every class
quick with the smartass right answer spoken out
of turn, shirttail untucked, sardonic lip curled even then.

He says that he's seen me on television
in Castine, Maine, in his assisted living.
He says that his wife is still in Philadelphia
and refuses even to consider moving to New England.
He wants to . . . what is it he wants to tell her?

That the curse of the Harpies is upon them,
that famine will force them to chew on the very tables
once spread for feasting? Weren't both of them
in my class when Miss Downes brought on the doves

that led Aeneas to the golden bough he needed
to get into the kingdom of the dead?
Juanita Mae Downes who never married.
Juanita Mae Downes, a graduate of Bryn Mawr
in the impoverished thirties, who saved my life with ablatives
and declensions there in the toilet stall, my feet pulled up
so no one entering the bathroom would notice.
He now in Castine, Maine, the wife still in Philadelphia.
All these sixty years fled. Miss Downes, be with me,

I am suffering from acute miserere, but who among us
would use it to call down mercy? Only your A+ students
and he was one of them, were allowed to read about
Dido and Aeneas making their illicit marriage bed
in the cave in Book IV. *Excess of love, to what lengths*
you drive our human hearts. And so he loves her
and leaves her. No mercy for Dido. None, we learn, has Dido
for herself. *I have lived, I have run to the finish the course*
that fortune gave me. I go to the dark, go gladly.

.　　　.　　　.

How I treasured my translation with your well done! printed across the top page in tidy red letters.

Let him yearn, in Castine, Maine. No mercy on his head.

MAGDA OF HOSPICE HOUSE

They call me Maggie here.
I love my work as specialist in easement.

Now I am naturalized and marketable.
Death is the thing I know, its catch and gurgle.

I oversee the art of dying—art
is what we try to make of it

with music and good wines,
old-fashioned beds as deep as cradles,

down pillows, percale sheets. And isn't it odd?
Juicy Fruit gum. I like to think

our ministrations, the bent straw slaking
morphine thirst, can alter history a little.

*I am so sad I have come out
on the other side,* the poet wrote

before he died, but all of us
one day will cross that boundary.

I crossed the Danube first on an inner tube
the summer of '89. My name was Magda then.

I was too full of empty deaths
to stay, too full of machine gunnings,

.   .   .

hangings, orphans unfed to the end,
bloodbaths in ancient Timisoara,

and then the tyrant's orders to shoot
into the swollen crowds in Bucharest. . . .

Nixon gave Ceausescu a Buick limousine!
I crossed to take my chances in

Yugoslavia—it was still Yugoslavia
back then—and gladly served six weeks' detention.

When Nikolai and Elena, hands bound, went down
before the firing squad I exulted.

Although I am faithless, I ♥ my new New York.
I can recite the "Stabat Mater," also Kaddish.

I love rocking my great bony babies
away in my arms, Demerol tucked in their cheeks,

or easing them onto the stallions' withers
and clapping them off for that final gallop

over the desert. O may we all come out
as softly dead as they on the other side.

GETTING THERE

in appreciation of Maxim Gorky at the
International Convention of Atheists, 1929

There is a special place that God has set
in Heaven for Good Atheists, my devout
fan Margaret's priestly brother assures.
I tell him I'm relieved to hear I might
get there. Judging from the surging hordes
in church, the public prayers at all events
since Satan brought the Towers down, there won't,
I think, be much of what you'd call a crowd.
Right now there's hardly anyone who dares
to disbelieve up front out loud.
So, Bernard Shaw and Maxim G.
save me a seat. I'm one with ye.

II

SEVEN CAVEATS IN MAY

When the dog whines at 5 a.m., do not
make your first mistake and let him out.
When he starts to bark in a furious tom-tom rhythm
and you can just discern a shadowy feinting

taking place under the distant hemlocks
do not seize the small sledge from the worktable and fly
out there in your nightgown and unlaced high
tops preparing to whack this, the ninth of its kind

in the last ten weeks, over the head
before it can quill your canine.
But it's not a porcupine: it's a big, black, angry
bear. Now your dog has put him up a tree

and plans to keep him there, a perfect
piece of work by any hound. Do not
run back and grab the manure fork
thinking you can keep the prongs

between you and the elevated bear long
enough to dart in and corral your critter.
Isn't it true bears come down slower
than they go up? Half an hour later do not

.   .   .

give up, go in the house and call the cops.
The dispatcher regrets having to report
there's no patrol car at this time, the state
police are covering. No doubt the nearest

trooper, wearing his Smokey Bear Stetson
is forty miles up the highway.
When your closest neighbor, big burly Smitty
works his way into his jeans and roars up

your dirt road in his four-wheel diesel truck
strides over the slash pile and hauls your hound back
(by now, you've thrown something on
over your not-quite-diaphanous nightgown)

do not forget to thank him with a six-pack.
Do not fail to take your feeders in on April One
despite the arriving birds' insistent clamor
and do not put them out again

until the first of December.

SUMMER MEDITATION

It isn't gunfire
that wakes me
but the rat-a-tat-tat
of hickory nuts raining
on the tin roof
of the trailer barn.
Then the barred owl
in the blackness, calling
for company, who
who cooks for you-u-u?
and suddenly
it's morning.

In the bathroom
the tiny phallic
night light
still flickers.
Black spots
of gnats, moths
folded in slumber
with one swipe
of the washcloth
reduce to powder.
An earwig to flush.
Two mosquitoes

lurking in the shower.
Killing before
breakfast

and killing after:
Japanese beetles
all green and coppery
fornicating on
the leafy tops
of the raspberries
piggybacked
triplets and foursomes
easy to flick
into soap suds.
Their glistening
drowning selves
a carpet of beads unstrung
spit Bad Buddhist!

At the pond
naked, pale
I slip between
two shores
of greenery
solitary
back in the murk

of womb while
there goes mr. big
the brookie
trailed by mrs. big
wispy silhouettes
darting in synchrony
past the deep pool
by the great rock

the great rock
that is always dark
on its underside
the one I used to dive
from, aiming to come up
in the heart
of a cold spring
rising exultant
time after time
into the fizz
of lime-green light. . . .

At sundown the horses'
winter hay arrives.
The dogs raise
an appropriate racket.
Always the annual

hay supply comes
at suppertime
on the hottest day
of August.

Eddy and Tim, oily
with sweat, grunt
bucking hay
heaving
40-lb. bales up
crisscrossed like
Pick-Up Sticks
so air can circulate.
They stand around after
holding their elbows
that noncommital
Yankee gesture
that says friendship
same as last year.
We chat, exchange
town gossip
the usual, except
Eddie's son
is in Iraq.

.   .   .

Afterward
the sweep-up.
Hay clings to everything
like rumor.
The full barn
cries summer, a scent
I suck into myself.
Big red sundown
induces melancholy.

I want to sing
of death unbruised.
Its smoothening.
I want to prepare
for death's arrival
in my life.
I want to be
an advanced thinker—
the will, the organ donation,
the power of attorney—
but when my old
dead horses come
running toward me
in a dream

healthy and halterless
—Gennie, Taboo, and Jack—
I take it back.

If only death could be
like going to the movies.
You get up afterward
and go out
saying, how was it?
Tell me, tell me how was it.

LEECH SPIT

For all the good it does, I apologize
coming and going, invariably forgetting
to take the long way round
knowing it isn't the same bird, only

the same way she swoops past me
all summer, less bird than bat, living
out in her encoded mother-wit
the same harsh sentence, already

sitting on her second clutch
of phoebe eggs in the sloppy nest
she barely bothers to remake
every May over the porch door

for no sooner has the last hatch
flapped to the telephone wire, still
beak-fed mashed mosquitoes, than
she's once again assigned to brood.

—

Halfway round the calendar
armored December lumbers into view
and the leaden four-o'clock sky opens
with snow squalls and bitter gusts

.   .   .

and every living thing takes cover:
small birds into the hemlocks, deer
to their pine-tented hollows
and in the pond, comatose

under the ice, leeches, aquatic worms
that thin the blood they suck from
their victims, thin it with their saliva
and it was leech spit, now synthesized

that saved me when heparin failed:
IV leech spit melting the blood
clot in my thigh so that in full-bore
winter, loving it, lusting in it I'm writing

this poem, confident that another
May looms for the dangerously
tilted nest over the porch door
I'll go in and out of, forgetting

to take the long way round.

THE APPARITION

True to his word, our vet
comes in late afternoon
and kneels in a slant of sun.
A pat, a needle stick
stills the failing heart.

We lower the ancient form
to the hemlock-shrouded grave
and before the hole is brimmed
set a layer of chicken wire
to guard against predators

so that the earth we broke
reforms, a mild mound.
The rock we place on top
common glacial granite
is mica-flecked and flat.

That night the old dog works
his way back up and out
gasping, salted with dirt
and barks his familiar bark
at the scribble-scratched back door.

.   .   .

I pull on shirt and pants
a Pavlovian response
and stumble half awake
downstairs to turn the knob
where something, some mortal stub

I swear I recognize:
some flap of ear or fur
swims out of nothingness
and brushes past me
into its rightful house.

THE SURVIVOR

Every cockroach is beautiful to its mother.

Neapolitan saying

Wherever cities are
she persists, a spurned lover.
Nowhere more familiar
is Black Flag, her killer—
the dead-of-night march
from Hell's Kitchen kitchens
from East Village cupboards
from dark holes in floorboards
to and from middens,
their mutual church.

And yet, The Little Flower's
mayoral deputy proclaimed
She rises hand in hand
with mankind on the long
long climb from savagery
to civilization.

At the eleventh hour
after the final hark ye, hark
after we all go under
she alone will lurk
hatching droplets of babies
to feed on the charred remains
of our apocalyptic blunder.

BROODY

Ideally, they like to get the hole dug, then lead
the crippled or blind or tottery ancient thing
to the edge and steady him with a final scoop
of grain before he topples, thanks to that one
well-placed bullet.
                            Last week a pickup truck
pulling a two-horse trailer went off the road
trapping two broken horses alive enough to scream.
No one could find a state trooper who would use his gun.
The nearest vet was on call twenty miles away.
You can imagine the rest.
                            So I said to her, Broody
every night when I checked for water and hay
and a decent layer of bedding, Broody
it's up to you. Stay as long as you like. And when
the thirty-five-year-old blind broodmare died
in her sleep, in her stall, in the night, everyone
agreed it was the perfect ending. But
getting her out wasn't pretty.
                            They had
to wrap chains around her hind legs and haul
her body out with the tractor, except she got
wedged in the doorway and by the time they had
pried her loose, her gut had burst and left
a fetid trail across the paddock—
                            for weeks

the others would stop to curl their upper lips
and sniff, heads raised in the flehmen gesture.
Even from the top of the pasture the herd could see
the backhoe digging and digging.
                                    It was March,
the ground grudgingly yielding frozen chunks.
The men grumbled at working in weather like this
even though they were neighbors, even though
they'd marveled a hundred times how she seemed to find
her way from barn to paddock to the back field
following the sun as it raised its curtain
and following the shadow it left coming down.

THE DOG OF HER LIFE

Acute kidney failure, the vet said, it can
present itself as suddenly as this, standing
across from her over the examining table where
each of them had a hand on the big dog to keep
him from leaping off in all his misery, Dog
who had to be dragged out of the car
hauled into the office, muzzled, and then
heaved onto the table for as little as
his annual distemper shot, his rabies renewal, or
the half dozen times he had to be put under
to extract the porcupine quills that ran
in rows down his throat, so deeply
had he bitten the enemy, and now
he needed to die so of course she gave
her consent to the lethal injection and
the two of them stood there softening
their holds, stroking—now that he could be
stroked—as he slipped away from them,

the vet of her dreams, as handsome as if
he had come from Central Casting, and she
slipped away, not in his all-white four-wheel-
drive truck outfitted for emergency house calls
but in her electric Toyota stopping only for
overnight plug-ins, metaphor intended,
East Coast to West Coast where they hopped

a freighter headed for Tasmania, a very
long journey she punctuated with epics of Dog,
the Dog of her Life, she called him, dreaming on
and as far as anyone knows they are
still travelling in one another's arms.

REQUIEM ON I-89

Crow pecks protein from the asphalt smear.
Woodchuck, muskrat, porcupine. The cousins
come. They strut, bicker over the impromptu
feast. Tire marks carry the stain
over the center line: bone shards, red fur
shreds of flesh up, up, up the food chain.
Such sated caws, such croaks of sorrow.

A mile down the median a deer
that chanced the metal barrier
—unforeseen by Darwin—between nature
and the internal combustion engine
lies on its side, burst open. The second
cousins arrive from hayfield, hedgerow.
Such sated caws, such croaks of sorrow.

WOMEN AND HORSES

After Auschwitz, to write a poem is barbaric.

Theodor Adorno

After Auschwitz: after ten of my father's kin—
the ones who stayed—starved, then were gassed in the
    camps.
After Vietnam, after Korea, Kuwait, Somalia, Haiti,
    Afghanistan.
After the Towers. This late in the life of our haplessly orbiting
    world
let us celebrate whatever scraps the muse, that naked child,
can pluck from the still-smoldering dumps.

If there's a lyre around, strike it! A body, stand back, give it
    air!
Let us have sparrows laying their eggs in bluebird boxes.
Let us have bluebirds insouciantly nesting elsewhere.
Lend us navel-bared teens, eyebrow- and nose-ringed
    prodigies
crumbling breakfast bagels over dogeared and jelly-smeared
    texts.
Allow the able-bodied among us to have steamy sex.

Let there be fat old ladies in flowery tent dresses at bridge
    tables.
Howling babies in dirty diapers and babies serenely at rest.
War and detente will go on, detente and renewed tearings
    asunder,

we can never break free from the dark and degrading past. Let us see life again, nevertheless, in the words of Isaac Babel *as a meadow over which women and horses wander.*

JACK

How pleasant the yellow butter
melting on white kernels, the meniscus
of red wine that coats the insides of our goblets

where we sit with sturdy friends as old as we are
after shucking the garden's last Silver Queen
and setting husks and stalks aside for the horses

the last two of our lives, still noble to look upon:
our first foal, now a bossy mare of 28
which calibrates to 84 in people years

and my chestnut gelding, not exactly a youngster
at 22. Every year, the end of summer
lazy and golden, invites grief and regret:

suddenly it's 1980, winter batters us,
winds strike like cruelty out of Dickens. Somehow
we have seven horses for six stalls. One of them,

a big-nosed roan gelding, calm as a president's portrait
lives in the rectangle that leads to the stalls. We call it
the motel lobby. Wise old campaigner, he dunks his

.   .   .

hay in the water bucket to soften it, then visits the others
who hang their heads over their Dutch doors. Sometimes
he sprawls out flat to nap in his commodious quarters.

That spring, in the bustle of grooming
and riding and shoeing, I remember I let him go
to a neighbor I thought was a friend, and the following

fall she sold him down the river. I meant to
but never did go looking for him, to buy him back
and now my old guilt is flooding this twilit table

my guilt is ghosting the candles that pale us to skeletons
the ones we must all become in an as yet unspecified order.
Oh Jack, tethered in what rough stall alone

did you remember that one good winter?

WHICH ONE

I eye the driver of the Chevrolet
pulsing beside me at a traffic light

the chrome-haired woman in the checkout line
chatting up the acned clerk

the clot of kids smoking on the sly
in the Mile-Hi Pizza parking lot

the meter reader, the roofer at work
next door, a senior citizen

stabbing the sidewalk with his three-pronged cane.
Which one of you discarded in a bag

—sealed with duct tape—in the middle of the road
three puppies four or five weeks old

who flung two kittens from a moving car
at midnight into a snowbank where

the person trailing you observed the leg
and tail of the calico one that lived,

.   .   .

and if not you, someone flossing her teeth
or watering his lawn across the street.

I look for you wherever I go.

APPROPRIATE TOOLS: AN ELEGY AND RANT

An elegy for the century I was born in
and outlasted somewhat to my surprise.
An elegy for the two world wars between which
I was born, an elegy for the sidewalk chalkmarks
I traced with my fingers, only years later coming
to understand that these meant a hot drink
sandwiches, an apple at the back door.

An elegy for my father's tears in 1939
over the final letters in his hand
from the desperate Polish cousins.
An elegy for my brothers who left me behind
the lone survivor into the 21st century.
An elegy for this century born in blood and bombs
and for the simple rights we once took for granted:

the right to speak out, congregate, sit down
go limp, sometimes get beaten up or tear-gassed
wait in the holding cell like expectant puppies
for the mother's milk of bail, next day
see ourselves on the local news, small heroes
or villains of nonviolent resistance fathered
by Thoreau and Gandhi

.   .   .

and furthered by Martin Luther King.
An elegy today for any who overstay their visas
which is now a crime against the state
thanks to the *Uniting and Strengthening America*
by Providing Appropriate Tools Required to
Intercept and Obstruct Terrorism Act,
for which the Patriot Act is acronym.

An elegy for our ignorance, for our indifference
to the fateful evening that the NYPD
—this is not a TV show—burst into
an Indian restaurant where two members of
Doctors Without Borders on leave were enjoying
a fiery green curry. Cops, guns cocked, screaming
kicking open doors to closets, to restrooms, the galley.
At first they appeared to be gangsters in uniform, but no.

They were checking IDs, seeking illegals.
The kitchen help—all Hispanics—
were made to crawl out on their hands and knees.
How else to witness their humiliation
except as malicious pleasure? No one was arrested here
but *I thought I had died and this was hell*
said the Egyptian married to an American,

.   .   .

father of a three-year-old, whose house was raided
in the middle of the night, a favorite Gestapo tactic.
Having overstayed his student visa, now a criminal act
under the Patriot legislation, he was taken in
for questioning, and declared an enemy combatant
not entitled to a lawyer or to a phone call,
but was disappeared into

a maximum security prison in the Midwest.
Released three months later, he faces deportation.
An elegy and rant for these and similar fetterings
that will reach none but the dissident few who happen
to read this page. Later, the words of this poem will be
swept up and discarded. Our letters of protest will be
shredded. Our legal channels will be cancelled.
If not blatantly rigged, our elections will be mishandled.

The man in the street will wave his allotted flag
and you there, without one, you with your publicly
negative e-mails and faxes, your weekly marches
which are still permitted but are herded into cul-de-sacs
where Mace and pepper spray may be employed
to curb the unruly, you are up against the wall now.
Up against the wall in the U.S. of A.

THE JEW ORDER

Mr. Welchon was a dusty, disappointed man.
He taught American History to my tenth-grade class
and was famous for his stringent pop quizzes.
The points of his shirt collars splayed out unhappily
on either side of his fat ties. Not a single girl
in the room had a crush on him.

This was an upscale high school in the suburbs
at a time when men wore suits and women skirts below the
    knee.
Because my mother was ambitious for me, I commuted
on two trolleys, an hour each way. Half of
the student body was Jewish, a quarter black.
The football team was salt and pepper, heavy on the pepper.

We yawned our way through the Civil War
the dates of battles, the burning of Atlanta
Sherman's march to the sea, the one black regiment
that fought on the Union side, the surrender at Appomattox.
Ulysses S. Grant, a splendid classsical name. We knew
he drank too much, that fact was in the history book

but not the Jew Order that he issued
out of Oxford, Mississippi, in 1862
expelling all Jews as a class from Union territory

in the Ohio and Mississippi valleys
within 24 hours of receipt of this command
for violating every regulation of trade.

Had we talked about how few Jews lived then
in the South, most of them merchants and traders
some of them daring to smuggle cotton up North
to bring in flour or shoes, salt or medicine
for the desperate Confederate households
risking death by hanging to slip past the blockade

had we heard, for example, of the woman in Richmond
before their dodgy shipments, being charged
$70 for a barrel of flour, who exclaimed, *My God!*
I have seven children! How am I to feed them all?
to whom the shopkeeper replied, *I do not know, Madam,*
unless you eat your children; young as we were

had we read further that any Jews who remained
would be held in confinement as prisoners
except that Morris Hoffman of St. Louis together
with his little cluster of B'nai B'rith brothers
threw themselves *on the bosom of our father, Abraham*
in the name of religious liberty and justice

.   .   .

asking him to annul that order and protect his
humblest constituents, wouldn't we have looked
at one another? Wouldn't we have felt the smallest spasm
of national pride when Lincoln said: *This protection
you shall have?* He revoked the Jew decree
the same month he signed the Emancipation.

Young as we were, had we read these two exchanges
wouldn't we have looked at one another
black kids at white and vice versa
sharing our adolescent fury at injustice
our radical innocence, our masturbatory guilt
wouldn't we all have looked at Mr. Welchon

who was there to teach and guide us in his boredom
he at the blackboard at the front of the room
we in our restless alphabetically integrated rows
for calling the roll, wouldn't we all
have looked at one another
with a heady momentary taste of solidarity?

INGE, IN REHAB

It hurts at first
sticking fingers down your throat.
Vomiting's an art
but after years of practice
I can do it now
just by thinking about it
the way some women can come
reading a sexy book.
It's like I open a door
and walk into a place that's mine
a place where I can look at
my knobby spine in the mirror
my breasts a guy I used to date
called little bee stings.
I haven't bled since I was sixteen.

I shoplift, too.
I don't know why I do it—
usually groceries
but sometimes jewelry
bathing suits and shoes.
I walk right out in anything
I like. The social worker
they make me see in here
says it's part of the same disease:
taking and putting back.

She tells me I need to
learn to love myself
but it's too late for that.
She tells me I need to
meditate, take up a hobby

but I already have one.
As soon as they let me out
I will eat till I overflow.
I will cram it in, two quarts
of Häagen-Dazs, two bags
of chips, handfuls of candy bars
and then I will throw it up
in plain English. I will puke.
I will barf like a dog who's eaten
godknowswhat, then stuffs
himself with grass. A dog
who heaves it up, then goes
back to the same old carcass.

LAST DAYS

We visit by phone as the morphine haze
retreats, late afternoon, most days.
Our mingled past is set against the pinhole lights
of cars cruising the blacked-out streets:

we four in the college smoker popping No-Doz,
honors students carrying heavy course loads
tipped sideways by sex, one by one discarding
our virginities on the altar of inverse pride,

ironing our blouses with Peter Pan collars
to wear on dates with those 90-day Wonders,
ensigns in training for the Second World War
in the Business School across the Charles River.

We called ourselves the Unholy Four.
Whenever any three of us met on campus
we huddled to bray *Austria! Russia! Prussia!*
in unison. It came out sounding like *Horseshit!*

Post graduation one year, look at us:
my new husband atop your even newer
one's car singing the bawdy verses
of "Roll Me Over" in a drunken tenor

.   .   .

while the scandalized uncles and aunties
—it wasn't enough that you'd wed a Chinese—
wrung their hands. You drove off
trailing *Just Married* in two languages.

Now BJ is gone, and Hettie. You have, they say,
only days. I want to go with you
as far as the border. I want to support you
this side of the *douane* and wave,

your two cats curled like commas beside you
as the barrier lifts and you drive on through.

HISTORIC BLACKSBURG, VIRGINIA

The lavatory sign still reads
Colored on one side and White
on the other in the old
caboose that used to trail
the ravelled skein of freight cars full
of West Virginia coal.
Whoever entered had to flip
his designation right side up
then brace against the track before
unbuttoning, back to the door
and pissing down the same foul hole.

THE HELP,

my mother called them in the thirties,
the burnished stream that flowed
into and around our lives, black
all black, she wouldn't suffer whites
to swab and sweep, Irish the worst.

Thus Lottie came on Mondays, whose
sharp-nosed iron opened darts,
vanquished wrinkles, force-fed starch
to the collars of my father's shirts;
once married to, long since divorced

from Fleet, who nevertheless
deftly held aloft the silver salver
of cheese puffs and chicken livers
wrapped in bacon at cocktail parties
the decibel level mounting as
the gin and bourbon levels plummeted

while Minnie, Bayou queen of the kitchen
every Friday bringing forth cornmeal-
breaded Crisco-deep-fried chicken
swore that only Clabber Girl
baking powder could elevate
her double-decker chocolate cakes.

.   .   .

Clifton, gay Clifton babied the lawn
barbered the hedges, crooned into bloom
the arbored roses, mounded black loam
around the crowning lips of peonies
his striped-red kerchief a distant bright bird
wherever he stretched or squatted down

and Hubert powered the Packard on
a dozen daily errands with the elan
his precious chauffeur's cap conveyed
ferrying the laundress, gardener, cook
and butler to and from the trolley stop
as well as his most important charge

Fräulein who lived in, exception to the rule,
governing the offspring who called her *Froy*
Froy wo bist du? in dual language school
but had her days off visiting her brother
taken prisoner in the First World War
now risen to downtown citizen butcher.

.   .   .

Such were the *help of the helpless, Lord,*
my helpful father peeling bills from
his folded-over rubber-banded hoard
paying under the table helping the help
out of helplessness himself out of his life
with the third and final heart attack

his widow reduced to one black
subsidized social securitied attendant.

CROSSING OVER

The living are not normally
allowed to visit the underworld
but in Book VI of the *Aeneid*
an exception is made:

Aeneas is led by the Sybil
through a series of hideous obstacles
across Lethe, past Cerberus,
to whom they throw cakes
of meal laced with the equivalents
of Valium and Nembutal
and finally arrive in Limbo, where
Aeneas finds his father Anchises

but cannot embrace him. *He tried*
three times to throw his arms around
his father's neck, three times the shade
untouched slipped through his hands
weightless as wind and fugitive as dream.

If only I too could undertake
this perilous journey with the Sybil
to see my warring brothers again,
who slipped through my hands
when alive, grasping and roaring

.   .   .

as if on opposing teams in the Superbowl,
docked for sacking the quarterback
after the ball was thrown, docked
for jumping the line before
the ball was snapped, docked
for the unnecessary roughness
that marked their lives and mine.

Let them slip through my hands
weightless as wind and fugitive as dream
bucking the line in Limbo
forever short of first down.

WHERE ANY OF US

Where any of us is
going in tomorrow's reckless Lexus is
the elemental mystery: despite

instructions he left behind, Houdin-
i, who could outwit
ropes and chains, padlocks and steam-

er trunks, could extricate
himself from underwater metal crates,
could send forth, he was certain,

a message from the other side,
never cracked the curtain
and Mary Baker Eddy's telephone

said to be hooked up in her crypt—
would it have been
innocence or arrogance,

such trust in the beyond?—
has, mythic, failed to ring. If
they knew the script

.   .   .   .

these two (God may be love
or not) they left, tightlipped
and unfulfilled.

As we will.

IV

—

THE BURNERS, THE BURIERS

Everything I leave behind me, burn unread
wrote Kafka to Max Brod.

Petrarch consigned a thousand
worksheets, he said, *to Vulcan for correction*

and Henry James in a fit of depression
burned his correspondence with

the magisterial Edith.
We might have lost

the whole *Aeneid* had Augustus
not overridden Virgil's

deathbed request. Plato as well
mistrusting his 2nd Epistle

declared
it should be set afire

but Alexander Pope asked everyone
to send his letters back again

so he could elaborate upon them
for publication.

.   .   .

When Prussian soldiers threatened
to storm the gates in 1871

Flaubert burned what was thought to be
a packet from Louise Colet

and far too hastily
Dante Gabriel Rossetti

griefstricken when
she overdosed on laudanum

buried all his yet
unpublished oeuvre with wife Elizabeth.

Seven years elapsed until
his want overtook his will.

Good friends then exhumed
his manuscript from her grisly room.

But it was the Russian poets who
knew how to dig a hole for, take a match to

.   .   .

hoard paper, make do
with scratches on a bar of soap

who smuggled out, besmirched and pied
their Cyrillics of rage and hope

excoriating lines we weep to read
yet leave them no less dead

Osip Mandelstam
sentenced for his Stalin epigram

Vasil Stus
buried with other *zeks*

along the Potma rail line
assigned a stone with number but no name.

So little rescued for posterity:
Everything I leave behind me, hold fast. Keep dry.

EATING BABIES

Think of setting sail from Tollesbury in Essex
for Sydney, Australia, in 1884.
You'd have to bully your way around Cape Horn
where 200 days a year the sea heaves up gale storms
known as the willawaws, thrusting you, mere specks
into God's hard hands from a yacht named *The Mignonette.*

A thousand miles from any landmass, you are swamped.
The yacht goes down in an instant to Davy Jones.
Barely time to scramble aboard the bare-bones
dinghy without any water or food except
for two tins of turnips you learn to love. Adrift
on day four you catch a small turtle. Nothing else floats by.

You are Dudley and Stephens and Brooks and skinny, shy
young Parker, your cabin boy, who, on the fifteenth day
gulps quantities of seawater to slake his thirst
and soon thereafter lies delirious, then comatose.
On the twentieth day two of you decide
that unless one is killed, all four of you will die.

You, Dudley and you, Stephens slit the cabin boy's throat
(Brooks dissents and does not participate)
and all three of you feed from his body and blood

for the next four days. Then you are rescued.
You are honor-bound to divulge what you have done.
After all, you are Englishmen, you serve the Crown.

Is this *Homicide founded on Necessity?*
You *put to death a weak and unoffending boy.*
Whether this be or be not murder the Court must say.
You, Dudley and you, Stephens are ordered to be hanged
but the Queen commutes your sentence to six months'
imprisonment, which you serve out gallantly.

Brooks gets off, it seems, although accounts vary, scot-free.
To preserve one's life is generally speaking a duty,
the Crown pronounced. *But it may be the plainest*
and highest duty to sacrifice it. Amen,
but is it one's highest duty on the high seas
to starve to death a thousand miles from land?

Examples abound: among the Aztec
history tells us, cannibalism was a necessity.
On Easter Island, man was the only large mammal
available. It wasn't so long ago that tribesmen
cooked and devoured two Peruvian traders.
In the pits of the Anasazi, in the Southwest

.   .   .

anthropologists have found bits of human flesh
in human feces. The Japanese are said to
have eaten POW's during World War II
and the starving Chinese—this may be a canard—
are reputed to supplement their impoverished diets
with fetuses. Shades of Dean Jonathan Swift!

Let us not overlook our very own Donner Party
whether they did or didn't. (They did.) But are we
to view cannibalism as always in extremis?
More than one tribe ate human flesh unapologetically;
fingers and toes were considered the choicest morsels.
What do we in the First World know of unappeasable
    hunger?

It's easy to satisfy lust; we eat, as we say, like pigs
greasy gourmands at the chain-food restaurants.
We're guilty of feeding chopped-up cattle parts
to fatten cattle for slaughter, and other acts
that go against nature. But what happens if we persist?
What if the environment so degrades that it can

no longer sustain the products we ask it to yield?
What if the water's not fit to drink, the sour fields
go sterile—sick steer, poisoned lambs, infertile hens

drive us to eating pigeons and rats, as in
Amsterdam, 1945? Then on to
killing and eating each other, like the Anasazi?

Imagine a time not far from our own:
we are the last species left that is able to breed
and eight out of ten of us now is born
with shrivelled lungs, a lollipop brain stem.
If you didn't know what you were eating at first
wouldn't your hungers drive you to taste?

Baby tongue, a delicious hors d'oeuvre, baby heart
lightly sauteed in baby fat, a substitute
for the now-vanished olive oil. Roast loin of baby . . .
And the famed law school case of *Regina
v. Dudley and Stephens and Brooks* will be
viewed as a quaint misstep, ancient legal history.

THE RAPIST SPEAKS: A PRISON INTERVIEW

A woman with a buzz cut
makes a lousy target.

I look for something I can nail—
braids, a ponytail—

and loose clothes that rip.
You're thinking *skintight* but

I prefer a flowing skirt.
I carry scissors for what's under it.

The perfect place to make a hit?
A grocery parking lot

or a public john.
You grab them going in

or let's say it's 6 a.m., she's on
her cell phone talking, walking along

or pawing through her purse at a bus stop
late at night, no pedestrians, no cop

.　　.　　.

let's say across from a park
ideal for a blitz attack. . . .

Just setting it up for you turns me on.
Even the State says I was born

this way. I used to get off watching porn
or trolling the suburbs, a peeping Tom

but life went from bad to worse.
Now I need to use force.

This time I had to kill to come.
Got enough? Take your notes and go home.

THE AGONY

He doesn't know where they are, the demented father
who murdered his children and buried them somewhere
along I-80, in sight of five or six sewer pipes
standing on end and a pile of weathered firewood
in Ohio or Illinois, Nebraska or Indiana, he'd say if he could
but reverently fashioned a cross of duct tape
that he stuck to the chest of each body before laying it down
in a makeshift grave he scratched in a grassy mound
near, best as he can remember, a yellow building. . . .

Still, he sent them off with the cross, that enduring
trope that comes into even a killer's head.
How the Crucifixion fascinates, is re-enacted
every Easter at Oberammergau where the spectacle
draws thousands of tourists. Sent to kindergarten
next door in the convent of the Sisters of St. Joseph, a little
Jew, I saw for the first time, in bas relief and color
a better than life-size crucified Christ at the end of
    the corridor,
a graven clay image time had let set and harden.

Who was he? what had he done? who put him there?
I did not dare raise my eyes above the next child's shoulder
for fear of having to look at that hanging man again
as we lined up for lunch, for recess, the toilet. I did not know

the word but learned it then: his agony became my agony.
Staying inside the outlines of sheep and boy Jesus we
colored and learned to print our names beneath. MAXINE.
The letters wavered, the N kept coming out backwards.
We also learned Hail Marys and to make the sign

of the cross to show respect and gratitude.
Can this be what my favorite baseball players mean
when they cross themselves, wet two fingers, blow a kiss
    skyward?
Tintoretto was paid two hundred and fifty ducats
for his wall-to-wall crucifixion scene, the Christ of worship
a spike through each palm, left foot over right
secured in place with a third, forming a graceful T
dead center of the painting while the strip-
mall bustle of the rest of the figures surge around him

in the quivering light and all of the other crucifixion scenes
of the Renaissance elders follow suit, but in truth palms
    would tear
and permit shoulders to collapse in on the chest and the
    Christ
would suffocate. *I put my hands in the nail-scarred hands of Jesus,*
goes the Baptist hymn, perpetuating the gore, but had they ever
seen an actual crucifixion, these Florentine painters? They

would have observed that spikes must be driven through
    wrists,
shoulders be roped to the crosspiece to prolong the agony,
    the agony

that leads to the Passion as it is told in the New Testament
which I never read until my late adolescence
in the Bible-and-Shakespeare course, a benevolent tyranny
exacted at Radcliffe my freshman year, and ever since
Sin. Good. Evil. Obedience. How to get saved from Hell
have travelled around with me, with Jesus and me as well
as with the murderer in the opening line of this poem,
a Nicaraguan orphan adopted at age ten
who will either be killed or imprisoned until he is dead.

May it please the court to appreciate that he is mad
and append a crucifix and a rosary to his name.

ON BEING ASKED DURING A NATIONAL CRISIS TO WRITE A POEM IN CELEBRATION OF THE BICENTENNIAL OF RALPH WALDO EMERSON

Caught up in a metaphorical swoon
by the oversoul in his head
War is on its last legs, he said.
The question is only How Soon.
Swayed by the cradling springs of his bed-
rock trust in the final perfec-
tibility of man, he elec-
ted Nature and found Her good.
This week a hunter sighting his gun
on a flock of ducks at that sacramental
hour when waterfowl season opens
said *pulling the trigger is transcendental.*

KEY WEST

This bulldog with a grizzled muzzle sits
from sundown till the last tourist departs
in the infant seat of a broken shopping cart.
Red-rimmed dark glasses are snubbed tight
with wires that run behind his ears.
He does a simple trick for our spare change.
His back is overlapping scabs of mange.
Still, why shouldn't he earn his keep? along
with this guy straddling a folding chair:
dirty jokes for fifty cents and up.

Against the curb, a body with a cup.
Why lie? its cardboard sign broadcasts.
I need a beer. A little farther on
another plays indifferent violin
two crumpled greenbacks in his open case
and a one-man band squeezes chords backed up
by synchronized bass drum foot-tap.

Heavy metal from the corner bar jack-
hammers its distortions down the block
throbbing so like a furious heart
that passersby can feel it underfoot.
Inside, on the beer-slopped bar's
TV, three more dead soldiers—ours.

.   .   .

The only female beggar on the strip
an all-but-brain-dead soul, once beautiful
offers each of us a baseball cap
of sleeping kittens. Ten dollars takes them all.
Where does she sleep at night? Who feeds her bliss?

They get by any way they can
panhandling up and down Duval.
You can't go any farther south than this
and still claim you're an American.

V

———

NOSTALGIA

on *A Shropshire Lad*

Lonely as a grasshopper on a hot afternoon
I fell in love at age fourteen
or thereabouts with Housman's lads.

Wedged in the beech tree's stolid crotch
I took them to me dying pure and young
lightfoot by brooks or fleet foot on sill

page by breviary page while snow fell
on Bredon (*o noisy bells be dumb*)
lugubrious romantic melancholic—

all those lost boys—faint echoes of
wars and wars ago, the Boers
no one remembers anymore

I so loved their sorrow notching my days
I have yet to let go.

MALE PRIVILEGE

To the younger poets, to be cleansed of envy

Wash from your hearts
all dark thoughts of me,
rinse free all memories
of my young worshippers,
sweet things eager to be bedded,
who would afterward
raise up on one elbow asking
at Bread Loaf or Sewanee,
at Aspen or Park City,
now tell me, what do you really
think of my poetry?

Soon I will fall silent,
my mind will wander,
I will read the same poem
twice in one reading
and fail to notice. I will
consume more martinis
than the fabled number
downed by Nemerov,
I will grow drunker
than Berryman, cruder
than Dickey, I will become
my own myth, they will remember
me for my outrageous behavior
and a few immortal poems.

ODE

Upside down and backward
windmilling through
sometimes satin sometimes

sullen murk, sun a tatted doily
intercut by overhanging pines
and hemlock, gliding

not too close to either
shore, water flowing
in and out of me

as I scoop deep
behind me, stroke
scoop and fling hands'-sprayfuls

straight-armed again and again
I salute you, Eleanor,
who outswam them all back-

stroking left right
somersault touch push off,
churning to the Olympic gold in 1932

.   .   .   .

ELEANOR HOLM
kicked off the team
in 1936 for drinking champagne

and shooting craps
in the first-class lounge with
Helen Hayes

aboard the SS *Manhattan*
I say ENCORE!
I raise a glass to you, Eleanor.

THE ZEN OF MOWING

How well I know
the litany of my long afternoon, the engine's lulling drone
   that slithers

under my earmuffs
as I glide on its steadfast thrum. How exactly I set the
   mower's inner wheel

so that it overlaps
the wavery lush first swipe I've cut across this late-September
   meadow

humped with
granite outcrops. The newly sharpened blade takes down
   milkweed, mullein,

thistle, purple
clover, Indian paintbrush, nettle, ragweed, late-summer asters,
   orchard

grass, timothy
in an effortless pass punctuated by an occasional stutter when
   the machine

.   .   .

encounters the
stubble of last year's sumac forcing a new tree up on the
    insistent root

of the old, for
even after the blade has severed them, every switch-like stalk
    is engaged

underground in
regrouping thread by thread, going on as we do, fiercely but
    soundlessly.

I look back.
I see not where I am going but where I have been. The
    stripes of my hard-

won greensward salute me. I sink into my zen.

FOR STANLEY, SOME LINES AT RANDOM

You, Sir, with the red snippers
who twice saw Halley's comet fly,
you, who can identify
Coprinus, chanterelle and sundry
others of the damp-woods fleet,
whose broadside "The Long Boat"
produced on handmade paper
woven from your discards—
here, the delivery boy declared
is Mr. Kunitz's laundry—
hangs in my study,

it's forty years since I, a guest
in your Provincetown retreat
arose from what you said
had once been e. e. cummings's bed
to breakfast on an omelet
fat with choice boletuses
that had erupted in
your three-tiered garden,
perhaps under one of your dahlias
the size of a dinner plate,
a garden that took decades to create.

.   .   .

Luck of the alphabet,
since 1961 we've leaned
against each other, spine
on spine, positioned thus.
Upright or slant, long may we stand
on shelves dusted or not
to be taken up by hands
that cherish us.

SONNET IN SO MANY WORDS

The time comes when it can't be said,
thinks Richard Dalloway, pocketing his
sixpence of change, and off he goes
holding a great bunch of white and red

roses against his chest, thinking himself
a man both blessed and doomed in wedlock
and Clarissa meanwhile thinking as he walks back
even between husband and wife a gulf. . . .

If these are Virginia and Leonard, are they not
also you and me taking up the coffee
grinder or scraping bits of omelet free
for the waiting dogs who salivate and sit?

Never to say what one feels. And yet
this is a love poem. Can you taste it?

NOTES

"New Hampshire, February 7, 2003": A blizzard that many came to call the Storm of the Century struck on this day in 1978. Much of the East Coast was paralyzed; New England was pounded with high winds for two days. Snowdrifts as high as fifteen feet were recorded and fifty-four people died.

"The Survivor": Fiorello La Guardia, mayor of New York City 1934–45, was affectionately known as The Little Flower.

"The Jew Order": I am indebted to Amina Sanchez of the Skirball Museum, Los Angeles, for supplying the exact wordage of Grant's decree.

"The Agony": Manuel Gehring, the man who murdered his children and fled with their bodies in July, 2003, was captured in California, brought back to New Hampshire, and jailed. While awaiting trial he hanged himself in his cell in February, 2004. The children's corpses have yet to be found.

"Leech Spit": Hirudin derives from *hirudo,* Latin for leech, used since antiquity in the practice of bloodletting. An anticoagulant peptide that occurs naturally in the leech's salivary glands, Hirudin is now produced as a recombinant molecule that acts as a thrombin antagonist.

ACKNOWLEDGMENTS

Some of these poems, a few in slightly different versions, or with different titles, have appeared in the following publications:

The Atlantic; *American Poetry Review*; *Court Green*; *Cumberland Poetry Review*; *Hotel Amerika*; *Hunger Mountain*; *Kalliope*; *Kestrel*; *Margie*; *New Letters*; *The Nation*; *The New Yorker*; *The New York Times Book Review*; *OnEarth*; *Pleiades*; *Poetry*; *Poetry Miscellany*; *Poets Against the War*; *Prairie Schooner*; *Rattle*; *Sheep Meadow Press Festschrift for Stanley Kunitz*; *Shenandoah*; *Smartish Pace*; *Texas Review*; *Water~Stone*